Dong Kingman

景

the water colors of

introduction by WILLIAM SAROYAN text by ALAN D. GRUSKIN

DONG KINGMAN

and how the artist works

THE STUDIO PUBLICATIONS, INC., IN ASSOCIATION WITH
THOMAS Y. CROWELL COMPANY, NEW YORK AND LONDON

MANUFACTURED IN THE UNITED STATES OF AMERICA

LIBRARY OF CONGRESS CATALOG CARD NUMBER 58-6611

1 2 3 4 5 6 7 8 9 10

Contents

Midtown Galleri

WATERFRONT ELECTION | *1956*

the eye and hand of Dong Kingman

William Saroyan

Collection, Mr. Cornelius V. Starr

SPRING IN THE PARK | *1953*

He looks at New York as no one else does—as no other painter, writer, composer, photographer looks at it, and of course New York is the world. That's where he is. That's where his looking at the world is steadiest. That's where he goes to sleep, and where he wakes up.

He really looks at the place, and he really sees it. Everybody whose business it is to look and see looks at New York and sees something different, perhaps new, perhaps important, perhaps special.

But I don't know anybody who sees what Dong Kingman sees, and I'll try to talk about it in just a moment. I've got to be very careful about it because in a thing like this it's easy to go off.

This is it, I think: he sees the world this instant, and in his glance, in the instantaneous and miraculous reality of matter and color, of living vision, of memory captured in the painter's great skill, he sees the world gone—forever. Not smitten to smithereens by silly explosives, not worn away by time and wind and decay, but gone forever in the very instant of its immediate reality—mixed, colorful, plain, heavy, but lighter than a man's soul, right there now and gone forever.

This quality in his city paintings is deeply moving, both delightful and sorrowing. We are not looking at a human face—eyes, nose, mouth. We are looking at the configuration and color—the mass of a place, a part of a city, a part of the world, that's all. Nothing of the human being himself is in the frame, and yet the picture in its entirety evokes The Human—gladly, and simultaneously with a stab of loneliness, longing, love, loss—irreparable loss—ache. The locomotive—what part of the soul, the heart, the hope, the memory of The Human is the locomotive? No one can answer that with accuracy, but the locomotive just naturally *is* some part of Man. It is not a locomotive as a locomotive is a locomotive on a railroad, in the heart of a city, on the waterfront, or out in the plains. And this has nothing at all to do with such literal relationships as lights being the equivalent of eyes, or anything like that. That sort of thing is trickery, and nonsense. Nothing in Dong Kingman's painting looks like something else, something it isn't. It looks like what it is. It's the *way* he paints that makes the thing painted—a traffic-signal arm, for instance—evoke a spiritual condition out of common experience.

You see, I have both got to guard against inaccuracy, and at the same time try to say as clearly as may be what Kingman does and has in his paintings.

Now, it has always been inevitable for the skilled painter of landscapes to achieve a quality of man's soul, in one or another of its dimensions, in the far-off turnings of streams upon the land, or the lonely grandeur of grasses and trees, human paths, roads, places, dwellings, and so on. The skilled landscaper of nature evokes in his paintings as a rule a lyric, or almost religious, quietude—nature's own far-off aloofness, serenity, anonymity, universality, and perhaps even indifference. Good landscapes are always good to look at. They do the eye and the heart, and possibly the mind, a lot of good. I won't ever be willing to knock a "View of Toledo," for instance. The clouds, the castle, the road, the wind, and the Greek's great skill are forever irresistible.

Collection, Mr. and Mrs. J. Kyle Spencer

THE CITY | *1956*

Collection, Kenneth Banghart

EAST RIVER | *1950*

Well, here's Dong Kingman holding an eye on the jungle and clutter of a city—an eye that's both microscopic and far-seeing—here he is holding that eye on a small patch of a vast city, an infinitely varied world, and by the miracle of his great skill, here he is making asphalt and steel, stone and glass, brick and board and iron and tin, streets and buildings, automobiles and trains, junk of all kinds—here he is making all of these things into an entity that is instantly real, forever gone, and somehow immortal, as if in his junk is man's monument, the image of his lost and indestructible soul. And this juxtaposition of rubbish and grandeur is just naturally beautiful. You look and you see, and you don't know why, but you're awfully glad about the whole business—man's proud futility, his brilliant failure, his heroic loneliness, his awareness of his end and his refusal to care about it. His refusal to stop in his tracks and let it all go. If he can't make a miracle, he can make locomotives. If he can't go to heaven, he *can* go to Hoboken.

He's an American, out of China, out of San Francisco. He's a wit. He tells some of the funniest stories anybody has ever told. His eyes twinkle with laughter and affection—for all things. All people. But never for an instant is he far from profound and steadfast earnestness. Perhaps even sorrow.

The foot of time, unpainted, without image, seems to be in each of his pictures. It is an enormous foot, vaster than the earth. It seems either to have just stepped upon everything, or about to do so. This foot of time seems to stamp the world as a side of beef is stamped by a Government Inspector, but there's no telling what the message is. Sometimes it seems to be The End, and then suddenly it's Forever, and then Now, and then The Beginning, and back and forth and all together, so that the sum of the feeling evoked is a mixture of New, Old, Ended, Started, Gone, Indestructible. Beautiful, and Tragic. And yet nothing he paints may be considered beautiful in any conventional sense. It's something, an assortment of things, made by man, seen every day, unnoticed every day, ignored, forgotten, much too familiar to be truly beautiful. But Kingman makes these things terribly beautiful. How does he do it? I doubt if he can say, and I know I can't.

The better part of any real work of art is essentially unaccountable. Still, it would be absurd not to understand that he does it by skill, by technical skill, by the skill of a painter. That is to say, he does a good part of it by skill—by eye and hand, paint and brush. The rest—the mystery—belongs to art, to human experience, to Kingman, to me, and to all of us. We don't know how he does it, but he does it, and that's what we care about.

He makes his paintings in a studio, on paper with paints and brushes. That's a fact, but there is another fact that can't be measured, weighed, or identified—the fact of how. How does he *really* do it? All great art appears to come from all men through one man. In one man it comes in one way, in another it comes in another. In still another it comes entirely from paint and brush, and you always know it, however cleverly the images and colors are arranged. There is a lot of good technical painting. There isn't a lot of painting that is good both technically and as true art.

Anything at all that is looked at carefully is worth seeing. Looking carefully makes it—whatever it is—a thing of fresh reality. The careful looking is the thing that does it. The act of careful looking, the event of seeing, is in itself the creation of beauty, and possibly truth, or at any rate meaning. But to look and to see, and then to be able to achieve the miraculous, the unaccountable, that is the true thing, the rare thing, the deeply moving thing, and that's exactly what Dong Kingman does in his paintings.

I believe I am a wiser man for having looked at a few of his paintings. I'm sure I'm a better writer for it, for the achievements of one art impel fresh achievements in another. This is my warm thanks to Dong Kingman.

Collection, First National City Bank, New York

GRAND CENTRAL | *1956*

TRIPLE DECKER | *1949*

Collection, Mr. and Mrs. Louis Kellner; courtesy Life *Magazine*

ANGEL SQUARE | *1951*

Collection, Mr. Harry Rudick; courtesy Time *Magazine*

Boston Museum of Fine Arts; courtesy Life *Magazi*

BLUE MOON | *1942*

the story of the artist

Alan D. Gruskin

THE CHAO PHRAYA, BANGKOK

Courtesy Fortune *Magazine*

BECAUSE OF THE NAME KINGMAN, MANY ADMIRERS OF THE WORKS of this noted painter are not cognizant of the artist's racial heritage, and the cultural and social background which has shaped his development as a painter. To understand how a mature artist's particular style has evolved, it is revealing to study the sources of the influences which have molded that style. *Dong,* when seen in print, might suggest some Oriental connotation, but the *Kingman* is usually misleading. Shortly after one of Dong Kingman's early exhibitions at the Midtown Galleries in New York, the artist received a letter from the late Henry L. Mencken, then at work on his *The American Language,* inquiring about the provenance of the name Dong Kingman. The artist hastened to explain to Mencken that *Dong* was his family name and, as was customary with Chinese, this surname was written first. Similarly, Chiang is the family name of Chiang Kai-shek. *King-man* was the artist's given name, which in this country had become Kingman and come to be regarded as the artist's surname.

Dong Kingman's Chinese parents were living in Oakland, California in 1911, when the embryonic artist was born. The parents had migrated to this country in 1900. Kingman was the second member of a family of eight children. Dong's father, tired of running his small, not too successful laundry in Oakland, decided to return to his native Hong Kong. There in the bustling activity of that great port of the Orient young Kingman grew up. His father was now involved in the running ot a successful department store. On the streets in front of the store passers-by were amused to see a young boy, chalk in hand, drawing large figures on the sidewalk. As the crowds gathered, they noticed the merchandise in the store, and many wandered in to buy.

From the very beginning there was no interest but art for young Kingman, and in his mother he had understanding and sympathetic encouragement. For years Kingman's mother had painted for her own enjoyment. As Kingman recalls, "Sometimes all day for a year she painted a bird in a bamboo tree. Then she tired of it. Then she painted another bird in another tree all day for a year." Kingman often sat painting with his mother, probably developing thereby much of the patience that was to be of such help in the later development of his technique. As that youthful talent became more and more obvious to his parents and neighbors, it was decided to send the youth to a Hong Kong branch of Lingnan University for advanced study.

There at Lingnan, Dong became adept at the ancient Chinese method of painting, copying day after day all the old Chinese masterpieces. Fortunately for Kingman's later career as a painter in America, he soon was attracted to an instructor who was a well-known Chinese painter. Sze-to Wai, with whom the student Kingman was to form a lifelong association, had studied in Paris and brought back with him many reproductions of the great French moderns, particularly Van Gogh and Cézanne, and several examples by Matisse. Kingman was much affected by these exciting approaches to art. His teacher, in the time-honored Oriental practice, invited two or three of his most promising students to the country to spend the summer vacation with him. Kingman, who was one of the students selected, made the most of the opportunity for serious concentrated study with a wise and sympathetic instructor.

San Francisco Museum of Art

WHITE SUN | *1940*

But when Kingman reached the age of eighteen, Dong senior, with remarkable prescience, came to the conclusion that the future for his son Kingman lay in the land of his birth. Kingman accordingly was shipped back to the United States, there to look for artistic and financial success. He continued his correspondence with Mr. Sze-to.

The year 1929 was not a very auspicious one in which to start an art career, or even to earn food and lodging; that went for San Francisco as much as anywhere else. Most artists in an America heading into the depression years were meeting great difficulties, which were to grow progressively worse. Opportunities for a young Chinese painter with little knowledge of English were particularly limited. But Kingman, with perseverance and ingenuity, struggled through the various jobs he managed to secure in San Francisco. Then for two years he was given employment in an overall factory run by a brother who had preceded him to this country. It was exhausting work, with no time nor energy left for painting.

Kingman had married a little Chinese girl before returning to the United States and she helped out their meager income by working in local sweatshops. Kingman's experience as proprietor of a Chinese restaurant, which he had purchased for $75, interrupted the series of jobs which followed his factory position. The artist kept an easel in the back of the restaurant; as a result the occasional customers found the service quite impossible. The proprietor was more interested in lingering over his paintings in the back room than in attending to the food and tables. The restaurant failed. Kingman's next stint was working as a houseboy. At a party some years ago I met the wife of an advertising executive who remembered the cheerful little houseboy who had served her family when she had lived in San Francisco.

Finally came the big opportunity in 1936, when the government, through the WPA (Works Progress Administration) program,

Collection, Pomona College

BIRDS FLY LOW | *1941*

enabled the artist to paint and, at the same time, eat. Young Kingman, who already had been showing occasionally in San Francisco group exhibitions and attracting favorable attention, now began to build up a reputation as an artist to be watched. His first solo exhibition at the Art Center in San Francisco was hailed by the city's art reviewers as a major event.

Junius Cravens, critic of the *San Francisco News,* wrote of Kingman's debut that the young Chinese artist "is showing twenty of the freshest, most satisfying watercolors that have been seen hereabouts in many a day. . . . Kingman already has developed that universal quality which may place a serious artist's work above the limitations of either racial characteristics or schools. Kingman's art belongs to the world-at-large of today." The "fluency" of the artist's color and the use of "broad telling masses" were favorably commented upon. Also at about this time, Alfred Frankenstein, respected art and music critic of the *San Francisco Chronicle* (long a Dong Kingman booster) was pleased to report in one of his columns that the artist had won the First Purchase Prize at the annual exhibition of the San Francisco Art Association.

Another important factor in Kingman's early career was the friendship and financial assistance of the influential San Francisco art patron Albert Bender. Mr. Bender bought dozens of Kingman's water colors, many of which he presented to the San Francisco museums to enrich their collections of American art. There was a great interest in the water color medium on the West Coast at the time and many excellent painters besides Kingman worked in that medium. Characterized by flat washes expertly controlled, these water colors brought those artists a reputation for having started a California school of water color painting. Kingman, with his Oriental training, handled this method with a mastery that brought him many of the top awards in various California regional shows. Then in 1940, from a touring exhibition of California artists' work, the Metropolitan Mu-

Museum of Modern Art, New York; gift of Albert M. Bender

FROM MY ROOF (SAN FRANCISCO) | *1941*

seum of Art purchased the first of the three Kingman paintings which are currently in their permanent collection.

In 1942 Dong Kingman emerged from the regional ranks to win a Guggenheim Fellowship. Kingman's project was to see and to paint America. The Guggenheim award, which enabled him for the first time to explore the vastness of the country, resulted in paintings of the mining towns of Nevada and Colorado, the busy streets of Chicago, the cornfields of Illinois, the mountains of Arizona, the charm of old New Orleans, and the still-careening "elevateds" of New York. This last subject was to become a part of the artist's repertoire for years, fortunately for New York. Kingman's paintings of the now departed elevated railways contribute vividly to the aesthetic record of a vanished era in that city.

Kingman was fascinated with New York. The elevated, the subway, the street and river traffic, the signs and hustle and bustle of the teeming city exhilarated him. While in New York Kingman formed a pleasant association with the Midtown Galleries group of contemporary American artists. As director of Midtown, the writer has come to know Dong Kingman well. Our close collaboration has existed now for over fifteen years. During his first visits to New York, with no studio available to him, Kingman would start his water colors outdoors, then bring them unfinished to my office. There, seated in a corner of the room, he would work away unperturbed by noise and interruptions, adding a color here, changing something there, as though he were solving some involved chess problem. And, for the record, Kingman is a good chess player. He is an expert tournament bridge player, too.

In New York, more color began to make its appearance in Kingman's heretofore rather monochromatic palette. The compositions became more involved, the flat washes of his early work were broken up, and forms took on greater solidity. There was more movement, sometimes provided by birds in flight. These birds came to be

Fort Wayne Museum

THE STORM | *1942*

Midtown Galleries

Dong Kingman with his painting, FROM MY ROOF, painted in San Francisco

almost a signature for the artist, just as antiquated autos were a distinguishing mark of his earlier pictures. A note of sly humor now entered his work, a strange, puckish good-natured humor that was to become more pronounced over the years.

Kingman's first New York exhibition at the Midtown Galleries was well received, and the young Californian was well on his way to national recognition. The winning of a second Guggenheim Fellowship enabled the artist to continue with his discovery of America. An award at the Art Institute of Chicago's International Exhibition and the Institute purchase of prize-winning "Passing Locomotive" was followed by the sale to the Boston Museum of Fine Arts of his widely reproduced painting of the sea, "Blue Moon." The University of Nebraska, the Wadsworth Museum at Hartford, and the Fine Arts Gallery of San Diego all bought Dong Kingman paintings for their collections. Each year the Midtown Galleries presented an annual Kingman exhibition, and the paintings were snapped up by eager collectors. Midtown also circuited a Kingman exhibition to museums throughout the country, and many of the museums participating retained paintings.

Many teaching offers resulted from the growing national interest in Kingman's work. The artist's pleasant manner with students, his serious interest in their progress, his charm and humor captivated those studying with him. And his lectures demonstrating his fabulous technical ability brought demands for demonstration lectures which have taken him to every section of the country. These opportunities have been so frequent that the artist has been booked for years in advance and has had to refuse many such requests.

In World War II, Uncle Sam beckoned. The ever-smiling little artist in G.I. fatigues was soon busily occupied at Camp Beale in California dashing off sketches of activities around the camp whenever army duties permitted him the leisure. Kingman had already executed an assignment for *Fortune*, a series of paintings of the San

Francisco war industry, and also had painted the activities at Solar Aircraft in San Diego. He was anxious to use his talent for the war effort. Finally, the government recognized that Dong Kingman's services could be used better elsewhere and he was shipped off to Washington, D.C., to the Office of Strategic Services. There he worked in an office producing charts and graphs explaining OSS secrets to government officials. Dong had hopes that eventually he would be shipped to the war front in the East as a war art correspondent, but the war ended with this ambition unsatisfied.

While in Washington with the OSS, Kingman was not satisfied only with office work. The city of Washington with all its wartime activity was available to his brush—and daylight saving helped. Consequently, Corporal Dong Kingman's 1945 exhibition in New York, later to be shown in Washington, included a series of water colors of the nation's capital.

When Kingman was in New York to attend the opening of this exhibition, he had a very amusing experience. Energetic as ever, he was up early Sunday morning to paint a water color of a subject he thought had good pictorial possibilities. At Fifty-third Street, near the Museum of Modern Art, he found a place deep under the arch of the Fifth Avenue Presbyterian Church. He unfolded the collapsible chair which he usually carries with him and began to sketch the disreputable rear view of the old buildings across the way. These contrasted sharply with the tall buildings of Rockefeller Center in the background. A motherly soul enjoying an early morning stroll stopped to watch the little uniformed painter at work. She edged closer and watched intently. Finally she could contain herself no longer. "Young man," she exclaimed enthusiastically, "you know, you have talent: I paint a little myself, and certainly can recognize it when I see it." Kingman smiled gratefully, and kept on with his work. "You should take advantage of the G.I. Bill of Rights and go to an art school when you get out of uniform," she insisted. With a

Metropolitan Museum of Art

OLD AND NEW | *1945*

35

Dong Kingman at his second exhibition
at the Midtown Galleries

NEW YORK AFTER THE STORM | *1942*

Collection, University of Nebraska

twinkle in his eyes, Kingman replied, "That is fine, but I do not like schools." The kindly lady shook her head sadly and walked away. The artist, after several hours of work, packed up the water color, which he was to finish in his studio. Later, under the title of "Old and New," that same picture was to be acquired for the collection of the Metropolitan Museum of Art.

Kingman's other water colors were also on the move. During the summer of 1945, the De Young Museum in San Francisco gave its native son a large comprehensive show and purchased his water color, "Nevada," out of the exhibition. The Colorado Springs Art Center, Cranbrook Academy, the University of Wisconsin, the Springfield Illinois Art Association, and the Davenport Municipal Art Gallery also bought Kingman water colors during the year. After illustrating an article on China for *Fortune* that same year, the artist was also invited to illustrate some books on Chinese subjects: a children's book, *China's Story,* by Enid La Monte Meadowcroft, published by Crowell in 1946, and Vanya Oakes's *Bamboo Gate,* published by Macmillan the same year. Years later, he was to do a series of charming illustrations for Hans Christian Andersen's *The Nightingale* for the Once Upon a Time Press.

After the war and his return to civilian life, Kingman began seriously to think of moving to New York, the city which was to play such an important part in the artist's future development. Each trip to New York had strengthened his desire to move east and to settle in New York. A writer from the *New Yorker* magazine, after interviewing Kingman for an article, wrote, "Dong is more enthusiastic about New York than anybody we ever met, Oriental or Occidental." "I am furious with color," he told the writer in typical Dong Kingman English. "New York surprised me. The subway so fast, so terrific. I like things in speed."

At every opportunity the artist had tried to record his reactions to New York, but he wanted to settle there and revel in the

One of the artist's illustrations from *China's Story* by Enid La Monte Meadowcroft

Dong Kingman in the Yosemite

material that attracted him so much. "When I arrived in the big city," he wrote, "I was not looking for anyone or anything at first, but because I have always been fascinated with city subjects, such as waterfronts, skyscrapers, subways, parks, etc., the first thing I did was to go down below and take a ride on the subway, going downtown and uptown, getting out occasionally to look and see. What did I see? Man-made monumental structures; dynamic streets and avenues; locomotives, buses; BMT, IRT, and IND—the fast and quick ways of transportation; the birds, pigeons and ducks; the animals, lions, monkeys, dogs, cats; the people—some happy and some sad; the atmosphere, noise, dirt, and odors. Summer is hot, winter is snow; subjects dirty or clean. I enjoy sketching in the asphalt jungle—the big city."

Dong, as he now was familiarly known everywhere, had given several demonstration lectures at Columbia University. These were so successful he was invited to give a regular class in water color. Then in 1948 he became a full-time instructor at Hunter College.

His wife and two boys were reluctant to move from the familiar Chinese atmosphere of San Francisco to the exciting but foreign and unknown New York. However, Dong finally won, and the family moved into a house in Brooklyn Heights, the interior of which, over the years, Dong has transformed into a handsome, contemporary, functional home and studio.

GRAND TETON #1 | *1947*

Collection, Atlanta Art Association

Now began the artist's very fruitful years as a painter in and of New York. The multiplicity of detail that has characterized his later work became more noticeably evident. All the objects that intrigued Kingman, the signs, the stop and go signals, the onrushing traffic, the gaping pedestrians, were woven into a richly colorful tapestry of a great metropolis, all definitely tied together with a sureness rarely seen in the water color medium. With his uncanny knowledge and by means of his arrangement of color areas he directed the eye of the onlooker through the intricacies of his design.

Nor was his very personal humor and whimsy neglected. As a matter of fact, they became more obvious, tinged at times with a little gentle satire. Strange animals lay hidden in the grass, and weird figures and statues appeared in the newer patterns. Traffic signs pointing in all directions, unrelated words, letters of the alphabet, and the ever-present cats were to be found in the Kingman water colors. In a *Time* article he was reported as having explained, "I put all that in for fun. If people take my work too seriously I am disappointed. Of course my pictures are sarcastic too. I mean, the signs say 'Go here, Go there' when you don't really have to; and on Sundays, when there is no traffic, the stoplights keep on blinking as if they were crazy. Don't you feel that way?"

Each series of paintings brought increased maturity, plaudits from the press and resultant encouragement, and financial success.

Howard Devree, art critic of *The New York Times,* in his review of Kingman's 1950 exhibition, gave such an illuminating description of the artist's work that I should like to quote it in full:

> Kingman's show at the Midtown Galleries is the liveliest watercolor event of the season. Better organized than any of his previous work, his overall designs incorporate bits of bright color and make fascinating use of forms such as old-fashioned street lamps, weighing machines, and clothes on lines as forms rather than as objective realities. His Brooklyn backyards are almost a montage of fences, rococoanut architecture, wash on the line,

WALL STREET | *1948*

Collection, Mr. Philip Hettleman

STREET
DONT
EAT
JOE

The artist in Milwaukee

glimpses of industrial details encroaching on a residential section, obsolete statues, and of course, the legendary tree, much deteriorated through urban hazards.

The openwork of elevated tracks provides patterns caught up for accent in slat benches and cut up by planes of light. Light and dark areas in the background are balanced as semi-abstract planes of form. Telephone wires cut across the view of a house by a roadside—a house grotesquely bearing several areas of different color paint—and space recessions are handled with sureness which adds to the spontaneity of his effects.

Kingman manages always in his own way to compass almost Marinesque panoramas of the city and its teeming waterways. Less intricate, in fact, simplified almost to the point of abstraction, he depicts the sketchy flight of steps on San Francisco's Telegraph Hill or a pile of timber left at loose ends for some unknown purpose by the waterfront. Almost out of the homely, disparate and so familiar as to go unobserved elements, he works out a compelling organization with a dominant mood, carefully selective of detail, and vitalizing the commonplace through fresh observation and rearrangement to suit the needs of his pictorial design. Forms, light, color are kept in balance in his stimulating interpretations.

In 1951 an opportunity was afforded to study the artist's growth over the past ten years. At that time Midtown presented a ten-year retrospective showing of the artist's work to celebrate Kingman's ten years of association with the Midtown group. Examples starting from 1941 included the early Museum of Modern Art's painting, the Boston Museum's "Blue Moon," the De Young Museum's "Nevada,"

A DAY IN CENTRAL PARK | *1949*

Collection, Mr. and Mrs. Jacob Bleibtreu

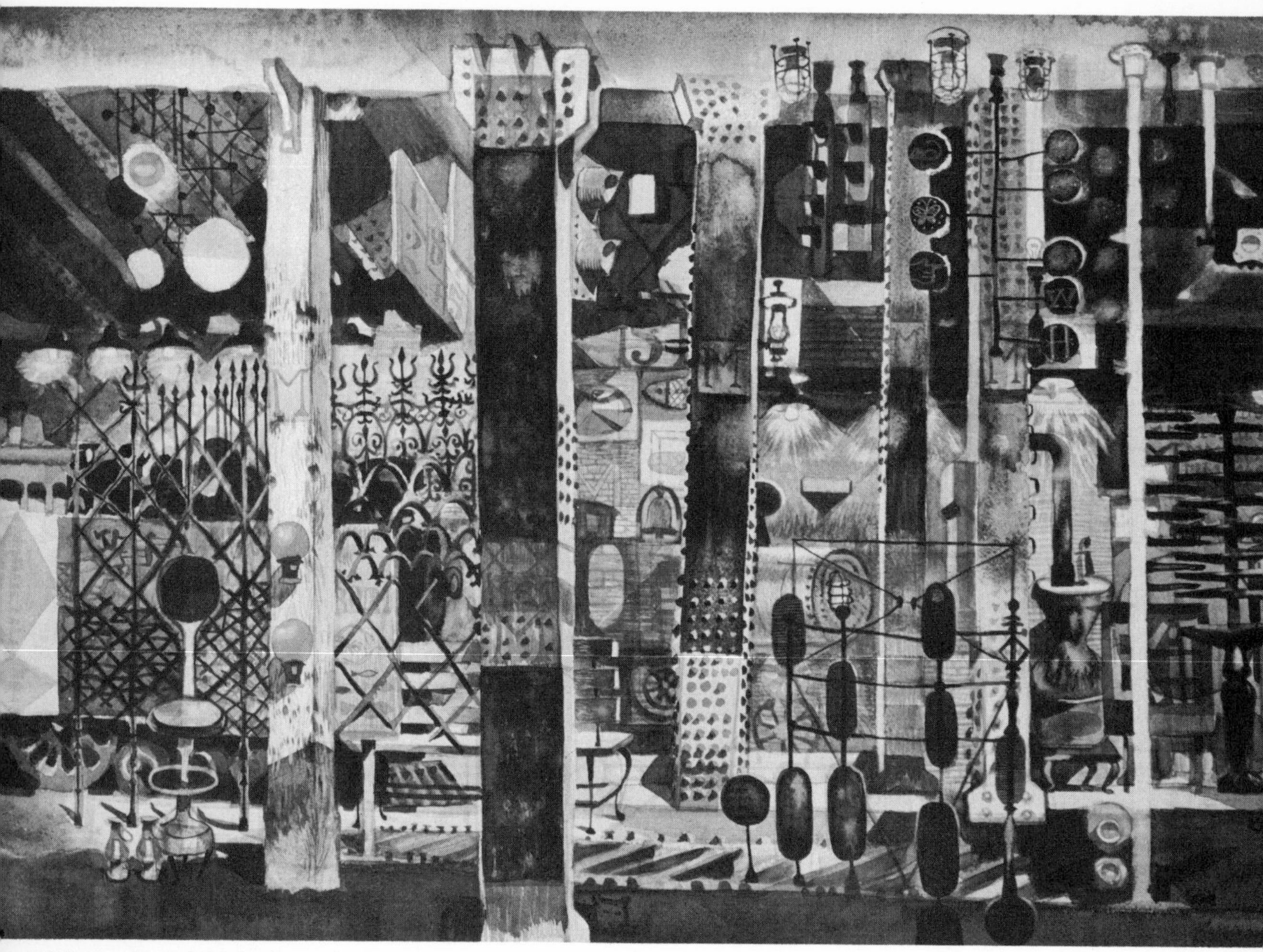

Collection, Mr. Ted Estabrook

STATION M | *1951*

and others traced the gradual changes in the artist's style, up to the large, elaborately detailed and compactly organized "Angel Square" reproduced in color in this book.

An undertaking which had its roots in a friendship formed in his youth in Hong Kong opened up new vistas for the artist. The friend, a Mr. Kenneth Chen whom he had met again later in San Francisco, was now in New York planning to open a new restaurant. Mr. Chen was a graduate of Lingnan University in Canton who had gotten his master's degree at New York University and had gone into Chinese consular service. When the Chinese Communists took over he was first secretary at the Chinese consulate in Turkey. He resigned and came to this country. He looked up his friend Dong Kingman and asked the artist to help him decorate the restaurant he was opening at 94th Street and Broadway. There was a large mural space available, for which the artist designed a typical Kingman subject, a scene of the East River looking from Brooklyn under the Brooklyn Bridge. Against the New York skyline, surrounded by tugboats, rides a red Chinese junk, the artist's version of East meeting West. The mural, twelve feet by sixteen feet, dominates the entrance and is visible through the street windows. It was executed in Duco lacquer, a method frequently used by some of the Mexican muralists. But the mural was only part of Kingman's efforts. He was responsible for the complete interior design, color, furniture, and even the restaurant's menus. He also had his friend Julio de Diego design some amusing and attractive wall fixtures and mobiles. The result was a very handsome modern restaurant with a suggestion of Chinese motifs. The Lingnan Restaurant, as it is fittingly named, is a far cry from the first Kingman restaurant in San Francisco, which went bankrupt. The restaurant came in for additional attention recently when the owner's wife, Maisie Chen, won $100,000 on a quiz program answering questions on baseball, of all things.

In 1953 the artist added to his reputation as one of the na-

Courtesy, Lingnan Restaurant

LINGNAN RESTAURANT MURAL

tion's top water-colorists by winning three of the major competitive awards in that medium. He won the $500 prize in a vast national exhibition at the Metropolitan Museum, a second prize at the American Watercolor Society annual—he had previously won a first—and the top prize at a Philadelphia annual national show.

Kingman's ambition to go back to the Orient had just missed fruition. He still wanted to return to visit the places he remembered as a youth to look at them again through the eyes of a mature painter. He had told the *Time* interviewer, "Everyone writes that my work is half East and half West, that I'm in between. I don't know. I just want to be myself. Sometimes I dream I'm in Hong Kong. I want to go back and see if the dream is right."

Kingman's wish was granted finally that year when the State Department, as a result of one of its happiest decisions, invited the artist to visit the Orient as a guest of the State Department's educational exchange program. Kingman was an excellent choice, for his successful career in the United States illustrated the opportunities available to an Oriental in this country. He also could effectively explain the great cultural interest in this country, of which most foreigners are totally unaware.

Preceding Kingman on his tour was a showing of the color film depicting the artist at work painting a water color. A previous film had been made by the Harmon Foundation. This new film, however, was a very professional job, photographed and directed by James Wong Howe, one of Hollywood's most famous movie cameramen. *Life* editor Tom Prideaux had written the commentary, spoken by the well-known Broadway actor Edmon Ryan. The camera followed the artist through New York streets until he found a painting subject in Chinatown. Then with excellent color shots it showed his method of painting a water color. The final scenes of the artist at home in his studio, living and eating with his family, effectively demonstrated the standard of living achieved by one Chinese artist in the United States.

An exhibition of Dong Kingman's water colors was shown at each stop on the artist's itinerary, which was expanded to take Kingman completely around the world.

State Department files record the artist's remarkable success, the excellent reaction to his appearances everywhere. Unfortunately, the beginning of the artist's trip was marred by the sad and untimely death of his wife in San Francisco. The State Department flew the artist back from the Philippines for the funeral. But with great courage, combined with Oriental fatalism, he forced himself to resume his itinerary. A record of his activities along the way, compiled from reports he sent back, gives some ideas of the ceaseless activity of this bustling little man. Some excerpts are revealing:

> In Seoul on April 27th and 28th Kingman did some mountain sketching [see reproduction, on page 54, of handsome Kingman painting, "Seoul," owned by Robert Clary], visited a high school where art is taught. Had many photographs and movies taken of him. On April 28th he went and talked with the Ambassador. On April 29th Kingman arrived in Pusan, where he exhibited his pictures at the embassy and spoke to a group of school children. In the afternoon of that same day he spoke with a group of local artists and met General Whitcomb, who came to see his show. On April 30th he sketched all morning with a local artist [painting "Pusan," on page 57]. In the afternoon Kingman went to visit a hospital. Then Mr. Kim, an artist, took him to a large pottery factory to make some black and white sketches.
>
> On Formosa he met Mr. Crain on May 17th. He was interviewed by the newspapers, opened his own exhibition at 9:30. Saw Mr. Nelos of the American Embassy, went to Formosa University and saw the Minister of Education, and visited an artist's studio. The next few days were spent sketching, going to the University, giving talks, and attending a reception.

In Korea, Kingman had the pleasant experience of meeting his older son, now in the Marines. In a jeep driven by his son Eddie, the artist rushed from place to place. Then on he flew. Crowds waited for him, holding large banners reading WELCOME DONG KINGMAN.

Collection, Mr. W. Alfred Hayes

VICTORIA MOUNTAIN | *1955*

THE BANK OF AMERICA, BANGKOK

University students crowded to see him and sat at his feet at informal discussions of art problems. After visiting various Japanese cities, he finally reached his native Hong Kong, went on to Singapore, Malaya, Bangkok, New Delhi, Istanbul, Vienna, Copenhagen, Oslo, London, and Reykjavik, then back to New York.

WATER TOWER, BANGKOK

"PEACE HALL," BANGKOK

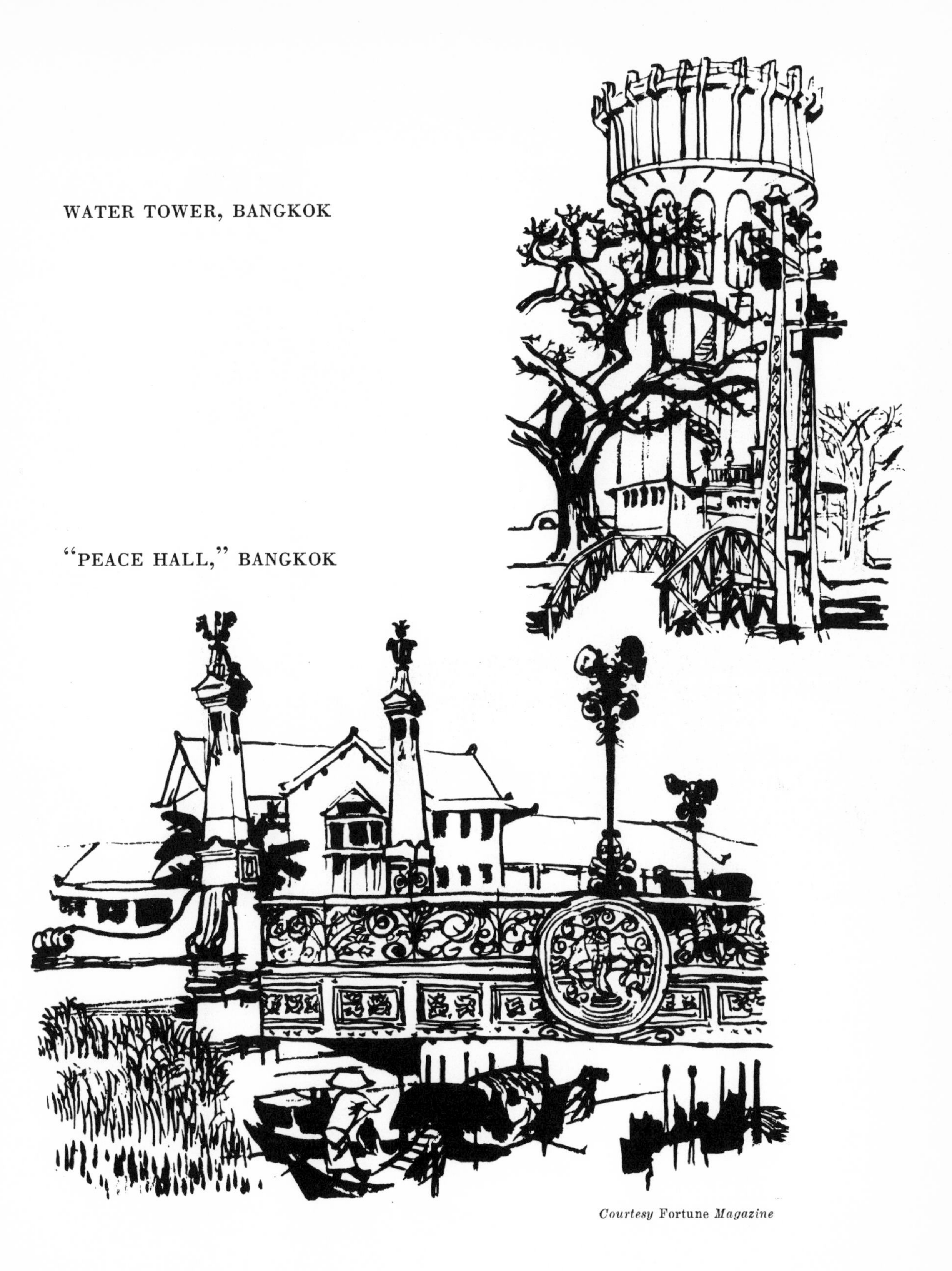

Courtesy Fortune *Magazine*

Collection, Mr. Robert Clary

SEOUL, KOREA | *1956*

Instead of the customary staid report of his journey to the State Department, the artist executed a pictorial résumé of his trip on a long Chinese scroll, which was later seen by millions in *Life* magazine's color illustrations. It undoubtedly was one of the wittiest, most humorous reports ever submitted to the dignified State Department. (See color plate, pages 126-127.)

The next few years saw ever-increasing activity on the part of the artist. He completed an assignment to illustrate an article on Thailand for *Fortune.* He had previously executed various assignments and covers for that magazine. He was invited to paint the cover for *The New York Times* supplement celebrating the three-hundredth anniversary of New York's founding. He later did a similar cover for *The New York Times* supplement on the occasion of the opening of the New York Coliseum.

He had transferred his teaching activities from Hunter College to the Famous Artists School at Westport, Connecticut, while still retaining his Saturday class at Columbia. And he was in constant demand for lecture demonstrations at art schools and art associations throughout the country.

The material gathered on his world trip was to furnish the artist with subject matter for years. He brought back with him dozens of his splendid brush drawings and many watercolors in various stages of completion, to be finished from memory in the privacy of his studio. Some of those on which he had spent more time painting on the spot were completed and sent off on a State Department-sponsored exhibition to those cities Dong had visited.

Among the recent pictures it has been interesting to note an occasional landscape, such as "Pig Head Mountain," "65 Birds and a Tree," and "17 Mile Drive, California," which showed that the artist still retained his Oriental influences. Some of his city subjects are beginning to evidence change. There seems to be less emphasis on the minute detail, more in building up simple massive areas. The

SINGAPORE | *1956*

Collection, Mr. and Mrs. Lawrence Buttenwieser

Collection, Miss L. Cohen

PUSAN | *1956*

Collection, Mrs. Chester A. Gash

65 BIRDS AND A TREE | *1955*

compositions are as involved but more subtly stated. His recent painting of New York Harbor, "The Helicopter," dealing with a subject he has often painted but never better, shows the artist's mastery in handling composition and evidences again his love for the city he has made his own. (See color plate, page 128.)

If his world tour enabled him to look again at New York with new perspective, it also gave the artist a taste for travel. He wanted another opportunity to get back to Hong Kong, to have a more leisurely stay there, to see friends, to visit with his two sisters who had remained there, and of course he wanted to paint the city. In 1956 Dong had married the beautiful and talented writer, Helena Kuo. Miss Kuo had studied at the University of Shanghai, and had managed to get out of China and write of her experiences in the book *I've Come a Long Way,* published by Appleton-Century-Crofts. She had worked for the U.S. Information Agency; had received a citation for her aid to our war effort; and had published, over the years, a series of other novels, short stories, and articles. She was a splendid companion for Dong Kingman when, in the summer of 1957, he embarked on another world tour that included a month in Hong Kong. Dong's stay in Hong Kong was a triumphant return of the native. Dong and his wife were guests in the palatial home of American businessman and art collector Cornelius V. Starr, who long had admired Kingman's water colors. The artist was interviewed by the local papers, and he and his wife lunched with the Governor's wife; but he also found time to visit with countless relatives. And day after day he was out painting, trying to put down on paper the beauty of this fabulous city. After Hong Kong, Kingman and his wife continued on their round-the-world tour. He painted everywhere, starting numerous water colors to be finished later in his studio. Rome and Paris had him working excitedly from morning until night. He arranged to be in London for the September opening of a show of paintings circuited by the State Department. With the United States

In London

Embassy officials attending and British officialdom invited, the setting was a perfect tribute to a youth born in a British colony (Hong Kong) and now acting as a cultural ambassador from the United States.

As Alfred Frankenstein wrote years ago in a foreword to a catalogue of the De Young Museum show, "Within a few short years Kingman has become one of our leading watercolor masters. One looks forward to his future with the assurance of one certain fact that whatever he does in the coming years will be quite as surprising as what he has done in the past."

Not yet 46, Dong Kingman has attained international recognition as one of America's major artists. With many years of work ahead of him, he should continue to add to his laurels, and through his personal contribution add to the importance of the water color medium.

In Paris (*left*) and Rome (*below*)

Midtown Galleries

TUGBOAT M | *1956*

paintings (1940-1957)

Museum of Modern Art, New York; gift of Edward M. M. Warburg

TRUCK YARD | *1940*

PASSING LOCOMOTIVE | *1942*

Art Institute of Chicago

M. H. de Young Memorial Museum

NEVADA | *1943*

Collection, San Jose State College

MARE ISLAND | *1945*

CHURCH STREET | *1945*

Collection, Mr. Edward W. Root

Collection, Addison Gallery of American

RED AND GREEN | *1945*

BACK YARDS | *1945*

Collection, Mr. and Mrs. A. D. Gruskin

THE FLATIRON BUILDING | *1945*

ection, Mr. Charles Stillman

Whitney Museum of American Art

THE EL AND SNOW | *1946*

ction, Mr. and Mrs. S. Berkson

WASHINGTON SQUARE | *1946*

Collection, Mr. Albert D

WASHINGTON MONUMENT | *1947*

CHATHAM SQUARE | *1947*

Collection, Munson-Williams-Proctor Institute

NEW YORK BRIDGE | *1948*

Collection, Mr. and Mrs. L. P. McKinley

Collection, Mr. and Mrs. Ben Shute

ATLANTA, GEORGIA | *1949*

HILADELPHIA | *1948*

llection, Dartmouth College

Collection, Mr. Edward F. Gamble

HOUSE NEAR THE RAILROAD | *1949*

Collection, Mr. George Fitch

THE FACTORY, ALABAMA | *1950*

BROOKLYN, U.S.A. | *1950*

Collection, Mrs. B. A. Lindheim

Collection, Mr. Wallace M. Cohen

BLACK BRIDGE | *1951*

ollection, Mrs. Samuel Miller

HOUSE ON FRANKLIN SQUARE | *1951*

BRIDGE AND WHITE BUILDING | *1951*

Collection, Miss Betsey Barton

Collection, Mr. and Mrs. W. R. Wilmer

WAITING | *1951*

Witte Memorial Museum, San Antonio

RED HOUSEBOAT | *1951*

U.N.? | *1951*

Collection, Mr. and Mrs. Hardy Maclay

Collection, Mr. J. W. Gratenstein

CIRCUS AND THE LADY | *1952*

Collection, Mr. and Mrs. L. Lubetkin

84

FULTON FISH MARKET | *1952*

Collection, Wilmington Society of Fine Arts

RAILROAD, OAKLAND | *1952*

Collection, Mrs. H. W. Glasgall

PIG HEAD MOUNTAIN | *1952*

SEVEN TREES AND A BRIDGE | *1952*

Collection, Mr. Henry Morgan

Toledo Museum of Art

NEW YORK HARBOR | *1953*

CHURCH ON CHURCH STREET | *1953*

Collection, Mr. William B. Lewis

Kingman

BUILDING ON SOUTH STREET | *1953*

Collection, Mr. and Mrs. M. K. Breslau

Collection, Mrs. Kenneth Montgomery

WHALE RIVER | *1954*

Collection, Mr. Abba Schwartz

PARK IN SNOW | *1954*

EL AND THE GREEN STATUE | *1954*

Collection, Dr. and Mrs. Mortimer N. Hyams

Collection, Miss Eve Hunter

GOLDEN GATE BRIDGE | *1954*

Collection, Mr. Lawrence Bloedel

SIGNAL WATCHER | *1954*

17 MILE DRIVE, CALIFORNIA | *1954*

Collection, Mr. and Mrs. H. L. Daugherty

Collection, Dr. Charles D. Lothridge

SOUTH STREET BRIDGE | *1955*

Metropolitan Museum of Art

Opposite: PICCADILLY CIRCUS | *1954*

Collection, Mr. Frank Picarello, Jr.

BOAT IN MALAYA | *1955*

Midtown Galleries

PIGSKIN GAME | *1955*

Midtown Galleries

COW AVENUE | *1956*

FACTORY X | *1955*

Collection, Mr. and Mrs. L. C. Kline

Collection, Mr. and Mrs. D. Norton-Taylor

VIEW OVER THE HUDSON | *1955*

Midtown Galleries

MOON & CO. | *1955*

Des Moines Art Center

BRIDGE AND GAS STATION | *1955*

THREE STATUES | *1956*

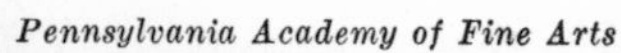
Pennsylvania Academy of Fine Arts

Collection, Mr. and Mrs. Peter Kriendler

EAST RIVER TUG | *1955*

UNDER THE EAST RIVER DRIVE | *1956*

Midtown Galleries

Columbus (Georgia) Museum of Arts and Crafts

THREE BUILDINGS | *1956*

DULUTH HARBOR | *1957*

Collection, University of Minnesota

Midtown Galleries

LOOKING NORTH, DULUTH | *1957*

the making of a water color

Dong Kingman

BOAT | *1957*

Collection, Mr. William Pahlmann

SOME PEOPLE, INCLUDING MANY EXPERIENCED PAINTERS, ARE afraid of water color. They think of it as a painting method that demands a fast and tricky approach. They consider it a most difficult medium because once the paint has been applied, corrections are hard if not impossible to make. On the other hand, many beginners, impressed by the deceptive simplicity that characterizes the finished results obtained by the skilled artist, attempt to paint in water color, and do so quite badly.

It is hard, of course, but the ability to learn the technical problems involved can be acquired if a serious attempt is made to grasp the fundamentals, and one is conscientious about applying himself to the task. Every medium is difficult—none harder to learn than the other—and, let's face it, there are no easy formulas, no quick short cuts. It should be understood that the learning does take years of work and constant practice.

As for myself, I have no rigid, no inflexible formula. I sketch as I see and feel, and paint whatever attracts my attention and seems suited to my brush. Sometimes I paint fast, sometimes slowly. It depends on subject, mood, and the effects I want to get.

My early study when I was a youth in China has unquestionably affected my approach to painting, and my thoughts, technique, and composition are often based on Chinese art and poetry. Yet today, after all my years of painting in this country, I feel that my work has little obvious Chinese influence. Developments in Western art over the past fifty years or more have affected my art considerably, and Western influences undoubtedly are now predominant.

Working in the water color medium continuously since 1931, I find it always fascinating. I also find that there is still much to learn. In all these years of constant practice, of never-ending learning, there is much satisfaction in the feeling that I can do almost anything I want with watercolor consistent with the potentialities and limitations of the medium. Any artists should feel that way about his chosen medium.

But in the last analysis this control of the medium still must always be secondary in importance. How you express yourself and what is behind your thoughts is of primary importance. Too many painters become skilled virtuosos, with little if anything personal to say.

Technical Notes

The following notes about fundamental techniques may be of interest to practicing painters and students. At their first lessons my students are always given instruction in drawing with brushes. Anyone who aspires to proficiency in water color should be able to draw with a brush with the same facility as with a pencil. Practice, practice, practice—there is no other way of learning how to draw or paint with a brush.

In China the first thing a student is taught is the use of a brush. All day long he uses it for writing words and for copying. Before he begins to paint, the use of the brush has already become second nature, or nearly so. Some people have the impression that Chinese paintings have little perspective or third-dimensional quality.

The artist in his New York studio

GRAND TETON. Water-color sketch.

On the contrary, one of the first things we learned in China was perspective. A good painting must have well ranged *yen* (dark) and *yong* (light) value, as well as third-dimensional qualities and proper composition. In China if one is painting a tree, the tree must have "four faces"; a rock has "three faces"; dimensions are referred to as "faces."

The Chinese artist also paints the object according to nature. In painting a tree, for instance, we must start with the trunk, then go to the branches, finally to the leaves, just as they grow in nature. A rock must be painted with a strong brush stroke, with a powerful stroke, imparting to it the effect of being hard as granite. On the other hand, when clouds are painted, the brush stroke movement is as smooth and easy as a ballet dancer. These rules are equally applicable in the West and the East. The only intelligent way of creating a drawing or water color is to start with the main structure and fill in the details later.

With a pencil, of course, you can erase; but not so with a brush and paint. Therefore it is important to start with a light color tone. Then in case of error, the work can be gone over. Much practice is required before the mixture of water and pigment can be controlled. Only after developing such control can one attain smooth and rough texture, light and dark color, and wet- and dry-brush technique. It is essential also to develop an ability to put on many layers of washes and still retain the transparency characteristic of the medium.

Materials

My students are given only eight or nine different colors to work with. They thus have a simple palette, and their colors harmonize easily. I give them still life setups on which to practice, for I feel that the mastery of technique and spontaneity are necessary before subject matter becomes the important objective.

There are more foto.
have been taken
of this subject.
so I paint it too
aug 27.54

I personally use three or four good, round sable water color brushes, small, medium, and large. Sometimes a Chinese brush is helpful too. I select about ten tubes of the best-made watercolors—I prefer the tube, as the paint remains fresher in it. My palette of colors is composed of the following:

CADMIUM YELLOW, CADMIUM ORANGE, CADMIUM RED, ALIZARIN CRIMSON, THALO BLUE, FRENCH ULTRAMARINE BLUE, THALO GREEN, BURNT SIENNA, AND IVORY BLACK

With these basic pigments I can mix almost any color or shade I desire. I keep the brush and tubes in a tin water color box. I carry a folding chair and a small water container, which are both kept in a knapsack. I ordinarily paint on one of two sizes, 15″ x 22″ or 22″ x 30″, using either a good, thick water color paper or water color board, for they are both easy to handle.

The White of the Water Color Paper

The white of the paper is important in painting a water color because of the transparency of the medium. It might be better if white pigment is not used at all for painting white tones or light colors, but the paper itself be used as white (see opposite). In other words, let the white of the paper show through. When putting colors on paper, one has to keep in mind the complete final result, remembering always that the medium is transparent. Layers and layers of color may be painted on top of each other as long as they are painted from light to dark. If light color is applied over dark, the result will be muddy or opaque.

In other media one can keep painting from light to dark, or vice versa. In building a house a man begins with the basement, and gradually, floor by floor, finishes the house. In water color the man must build the whole house—basement, first, second, and third floor, simultaneously.

STREET SCENE, SALZBURG. Water-color sketch.

Collection, Mr. F. T. Forster

COLUMBUS CIRCLE | *1942*

It is a common belief that the water color medium is a quick, spontaneous method of painting, and that no revisions can be made without ruining the paper and losing the freshness characteristic of the medium. I have found through years of experience, and with the exercise of considerable care and patience, that water color can be kept fresh and sparkling, and the paper kept in good condition despite constant changes and revisions. I compose on the paper, wiping out and changing various areas of the picture as I progress, often working months on a water color—sometimes years. Wiping off can be done with a clean rag or with soft paper handkerchief tissues.

Here are some notes made in my diary about the painting "Columbus Circle" (reproduced on page 122):

> On October 15, 1942 it was a very nice Thursday morning when I decided to go out to Central Park to look for a subject to paint. Birds were singing and the trees began turning beautiful shades of orange and yellow, making a wonderful panorama of color. I just ambled along until I came to the vicinity of Columbus Circle and 59th Street. There I saw the monument to Columbus, and I found it a very interesting subject. Deciding that this was what I was looking for, I proceeded to do a very rough pencil sketch of it. I then went back to my studio and studied it in a number of brush sketches, coming to the conclusion that it would be a good thing to develop. And so, on October 18 (Sunday morning), at 8 o'clock, after gulping a cup of coffee, I got my things ready, went down to the Park, and started to work, using my sketch pad, and working in brush lines with very light water-color of no particular shade. I lowered the buildings so the monument would rise against the dark sky as it was very beautiful this way. I also changed the buildings to suit the composition I had previously developed in my studio studies, doing this until I got exactly what I wanted. Soon a large audience of curious bystanders had congregated, among whom was a man who loved pigeons. He showed it by sprinkling bread not only on the birds but on me, my picture, and all my paints!
>
> I then put aside the bread crumbs, my sketch pad, got out my water-color paper, and in very light brush lines copied what I had produced on the sketch pad.
>
> Now I had to work on my values, and so I laid a light wash of color on the picture to indicate the strong values, and then I had to wait for it to dry, giving my audience the impression that all was finished. But they were

wrong, for I had just begun. Now I had a rough idea of my dark and light values, so I began with the color, trying to make it as powerful as the dark should be, and as light as it should be, concentrating on the picture as a whole. After I had the monument and the street lights, a few people here and there, some of the buildings and the background, I then proceeded to lay in the sky, after which I worked, in detail, the rest of the picture. I had not yet put the shadows in when a few drops of rain came, causing me to go back to my studio, which was just as well because many of my pictures are completed indoors anyhow.

The Helicopter (Page 128)

One late afternoon in the summer not so long ago, I was walking in downtown Manhattan all by myself. Suddenly the storm clouds gathered and the sky hung low. I looked around for shelter, and there standing before my eyes was a full view of three giant bridges: the Manhattan, the Brooklyn, and the Williamsburg.

What a wonderful subject this is for a painting, I said to myself. And what weather! The power, the vitality, and the intricate pattern of the city architecture all woven together. I could not wait to get my collapsible stool and painting equipment to put all this down on paper.

Early next morning, when the city was still half asleep and there was practically no traffic, I dashed back to the scene—Pier 6 on the East River. From there, the magnificent view of the three bridges interwoven with Manhattan's skyscrapers on the left and the Navy Yard in Brooklyn on the right unfolded before my eyes. Here and there on the rippling surface of the water were tugboats and steamers trolling lazily by. I knew then I had found *the spot.* The picture I painted is shown in color on page 128.

How I Began My Painting. Locating the subject is, of course, an important step in beginning a picture. My next step is to sit myself down as comfortably as possible on the collapsible stool and lay out my water color equipment. I was ready for action.

Collection, Mr. Stanley Barbee; courtesy Time *Magazine*

MOON AND LOCOMOTIVE | *1952*

July 25TH 7P.M.
arrived
Penang
EXHIBITION
And then took a
fly up to
Bangkok.
泰國
arrived July 29
August 7TH
midnight
arrived Delhi
India
a cow were
sitting around
just eating
up time (newspaper)
On aug 13TH took a train
EXHIBIT

Courtesy Life Magazine

SCROLL PAINTING (Report to State Department)

Midtown Galleries

THE HELICOPTER | *1957*

A painter's eyes must see what another person does not see. They must be able to absorb what is good for a picture and what is not. With brush in hand and a 22 x 29-inch piece of 300-pound water-color paper in front, I was ready to put down a few brief lines to indicate the center of interest for the picture.

I wetted my brush and worked with the colors—learning what to put in and what to leave out as I went along. It generally takes two to three hours, or a good part of the morning, for me to put down the essential parts of the scenery in a picture, the surrounding areas to be finished later in the studio.

I also believe in sketching and painting the actual subjects on the spot, as this is the way, the only way, to feel the atmosphere around and to capture the mood right there on location.

The Composition. Every artist has his own method of working. My method, of course, is what I have developed for myself. My picture is generally 25 to 40 percent finished on location.

For me, it is always better to have the semifinished picture hanging around the studio for a while. This gives me an opportunity to study and to plan more carefully before completion.

Looking at the unfinished picture on the easel, I may make many preliminary sketches, with as many different ideas, to experiment with the colors and the tonal values.

In Diagram A (page 130) for instance, I experimented with a dark color for the sea and a light color for the sky, while the tugboats move along the lower left-hand corner.

In Diagram B, I experimented with dark backgrounds and light tone for the top and foreground of the picture and with noticeable spotlights on the pier.

But I decided to settle for Diagram C, which final and effective result you can see in the color reproduction on page 128.

One lesson I have learned in my years of painting is that it would be distracting to have a direct line, or lines, cut across the top

Diagram A

Preliminary sketches for THE HELICOPTER, reproduced on page 128

Diagram B

The last preliminary sketch

of a picture, or for that matter, across any part of a picture. To stop the line of the bridge from cutting across the picture, I placed a perpendicular building on the left-hand side in front of the bridge.

You may notice the square area at the top of the bridge on the upper right-hand corner. I had put it there on purpose. I was thinking, at first, of hanging a sheet of cloth, or a towel, over the bridge. But when I studied more of the composition of the painting, as experimented in both Diagrams A and B, I came to the conclusion that I should put a helicopter there instead, if I were to complete the picture according to Diagram C—with the top part of the picture very dark, expressing the threatening storm, and the lower part in light colors for the churning sea.

If you should ask why I put a statue instead of a tugboat on the lower right-hand corner, my answer is that I like to give the feeling of being in an open park in the picture. And who doesn't enjoy being in an open park?

And why the wooden ducks in the foreground? Well, they are for the fishermen when they go fishing. This is a picture of the waterfront, remember?

A Closing Thought. One must learn all he can about the handling of the brush, the choice of colors, the tonal values, the use of techniques, and all the necessary tools and knowledge to become an artist. But that is only the beginning. An artist must continue to search—for himself, and for something which is always there but may not be there.

One may continue to search, on and on. But he does not have to straddle heavily and clumsily along the way. He can enjoy the task of painting, because painting *is* fun.

Midtown Galleries

PHILIPPINE ISLANDS | *1954*

Arthur Eckstein

James Wong Howe photographing Dong Kingman for an educational film

index to collections

Water colors by Dong Kingman may be seen in any of the following public collections.

CALIFORNIA	
OAKLAND:	*Mills College*
POMONA:	*Los Angeles County Fair Association*
SAN DIEGO:	*San Diego Fine Arts Gallery*
SAN JOSE:	*San Jose State College*
SAN FRANCISCO:	*M. H. de Young Memorial Museum*
	San Francisco Museum
CONNECTICUT	
HARTFORD:	*Wadsworth Atheneum*
NEW BRITAIN:	*Art Museum of New Britain*
DELAWARE	
WILMINGTON:	*Wilmington Society of Fine Arts*
DISTRICT OF COLUMBIA	
WASHINGTON:	*Department of State*
GEORGIA	
ATLANTA:	*Atlanta Art Association*
COLUMBUS:	*Columbus Museum of Arts and Crafts*
ILLINOIS	
BLOOMINGTON:	*Bloomington Art Association*
CHICAGO:	*The Art Institute of Chicago*
SPRINGFIELD:	*Springfield Art Association*
INDIANA	
EVANSVILLE:	*Evansville Public Museum*
FORT WAYNE:	*Fort Wayne Art School and Museum*

IOWA

DAVENPORT:	*Davenport Municipal Gallery*
DES MOINES:	*Des Moines Art Center*

MASSACHUSETTS

ANDOVER:	*Addison Gallery of American Art*
BOSTON:	*Museum of Fine Arts*

MICHIGAN

BLOOMFIELD HILLS:	*Cranbrook Academy of Art*

MINNESOTA

DULUTH:	*University of Minnesota*

NEBRASKA

LINCOLN:	*University of Nebraska*

NEW HAMPSHIRE

HANOVER:	*Dartmouth College*

NEW YORK

BROOKLYN:	*Brooklyn Museum of Art*
NEW YORK:	*American Academy of Arts and Letters*
	Metropolitan Museum of Art
	Museum of Modern Art
	National Academy of Design
	Whitney Museum of American Art
OSWEGO:	*State Teachers College*
UTICA:	*Munson-Williams-Proctor Institute*

OHIO

TOLEDO:	*Toledo Museum of Art*
YOUNGSTOWN:	*The Butler Art Institute*

PENNSYLVANIA

PHILADELPHIA:	*Pennsylvania Academy of Fine Arts*
STATE COLLEGE:	*Pennsylvania State College*

TEXAS

SAN ANTONIO:	*Witte Memorial Museum*

WISCONSIN

MADISON:	*University of Wisconsin*